Carryin

Sian Allen

BookLeaf
Publishing

Presentation by *BookLeaf Publishing*

Web: www.bookleafpub.com

E-mail: info@bookleafpub.com

ISBN: 9789395620901

First edition 2022

DEDICATION

This collection is dedicated to Wilf, forever my inspiration.

ACKNOWLEDGEMENT

Thanks to Steven, who supported me on this journey of becoming a mother and embarking on this challenge.

PREFACE

Research completed at the University of Essex (2022) found that post-pandemic, the anxiety rates of UK expectant mothers increased from 37% to 60%.

We need to stand together, support one another and SPEAK UP about our mental health. It's okay not to be okay!

This book was written with acknowledgment of both the struggles and beauty of creating a life. That not every day is easy, but every day is a step forward.

Positive

one strong line
then another,
slight but there

blink
blink again,
why can't I breathe?

one test, two tests,
three tests, four.
all show the same through the tears:

I'm p r e g n a n t.

Stretch Marks

linear traces over the globe
that was my stomach,
I will grow with you

Nine Months

nine months to hold you,
a distant thought that will grow
from a cell
to my boy in blue

to the man that you'll become

Turning

bottom cocked moonward,
an ode to leaving the stars:
now he kicks to them

a gentle acknowledgment

Who Are You?

you're mine, yet unfamiliar;
a face I've never seen before.
there's days that I don't recognise my own

Wondering

I can't help but wonder

do you have thoughts,
can you feel what I feel?

can you hear my smile
or taste the salt when I cry?

can you feel the gravitational pull
bringing you closer to your earthly start?

Mother Tongue

a soft voice to lull and comfort:
syllables to recognise,
your mother tongue

Change

the world turns fast under my feet,
like greeting the premature change of seasons.
thick frost thaws too quickly into spring time,
sprouting flowers. they look up and beg for
warmth.
the summer breeze then sings it's odes to
Autumn,
bringing down crunchy leaves of red and orange
somehow ready to drop

Hyperemesis

one bucket near to the bed,
two bitter tasting paracetamol
with an iced bottle of water
gone warm.
three plain crackers
is all we'll manage today,
swallowed down with
a distant hope tomorrow will be better.

What's A Newborn?

a newborn is

the deep suckle of a breast
in hours of the night you didn't realise exist.
a sweet smelling dream:
pinch yourself, you're awake.
a thousand cries, ten thousand nappies,
outshone by one unforgettable moon-faced
smile.

a newborn is
a reach out
for your love

admitting that
you need them too

Baking Baby

- 2 sweet kisses
- an ounce of sugar
- only one pinch of salt
- chopped leafy greens
you really don't want
- 2 hearts beating close by
(yours and mine)
- a sprinkling of folic acid
- don't forget a few teardrops
- a small shiver of excitement
sifted through with the unknown

when baked
serve warm
wrap neatly
love fearlessly

I Am

I am
a milk producer,
a cradler,
a comforter.

I am
a walking sacrifice
of all I chose
to leave behind.

I am
counting down the seconds
until I can hold you
and kiss those tiny hands.

I am finding
my true self:
being your mother.

Laundry

machine set to delicates,
a mighty mission:
surge through a mountain
of baby whites and
tiny woollen knits
fit to measure a doll.
soapy suds swirl,
the rhythmic spinning lulls me
to another place.
the smell of spilled comfort
stays on my hands all day.

Anticipating

pain pulsating,
angry black waves
twist me head to toe

back arching
ears ringing
a thousand hornets

keep thinking
each sting is
one closer

to holding you

Nine Days

once nine months, now down to days
what seemed like a lifetime to wait
now down to hours, minutes, seconds.
Like a child counting down to Christmas,
wonder and hope reflect as lights in my eyes.

Nine days until we meet you,
hold you.
our whirlwind
our dream come true

Home

I'll hold you close when you laugh,
when you turn to cry.
my open arms are your home,
just as you are mine.

Your Arrival

how will it feel,
my empty body, aching.
how will it feel,
grasping my tiny,
wrinkled, crying new arrival.

a fresh slate, a new start
that smells like baby powder.
will it be like looking out over
a calm, lapping sea at sunset,
or will your tide be ferocious?

Mother

I am your mother,
your guardian, your safe place.
I will watch as you run

and smile, remembering
these precious early days.
I'll cherish them like diamonds